What's in this book

This book belongs to

T0351520

_____

我们一起玩 Let's all play

学习内容 Contents

沟通 Communication

称呼家庭成员
Address family members

背景介绍：
浩浩和玲玲拿出了一副棋盘游戏。

生词 New words

★	爸爸	father, dad
★	妈妈	mother, mum
★	姐姐	elder sister
★	弟弟	younger brother
★	狗	dog
	和	and
	一起	together
	玩	to play

姐姐和弟弟一起玩。
The elder sister and the younger brother play together.

跨学科学习 Project

制作家谱，介绍家庭成员
Make a family tree and describe your family members

文化 Cultures

中国家庭亲属称谓
Chinese kinship terms

参考答案：
1 Yes, I have a dog./No, I do not have any pets.
2 My favourite family activity is playing badminton.
3 They are going to play a board game.

Get ready

1 Do you have any pets?

2 What is your favourite family activity?

3 What is Hao Hao's family going to play?

故事大意：
浩浩一家玩棋盘游戏，连布朗尼也参与了进来。

bà ba
爸爸

爸爸和我们一起玩。

我们用"和"来连接
并列的人、事、物。

参考问题和答案：

1 Who is playing the board game with Hao Hao and Ling Ling? (Dad.)

2 Whose turn is it? (It is Dad's turn.)

3 How do they look? (They look happy.)

4

姐姐和我一起玩。

提醒学生，这句话是以浩浩的视角说的。

参考问题和答案：

1 Whose turn is it? (It is Ling Ling's turn. She is Hao Hao's sister.)
2 What is Mum doing? (She is walking to the kitchen.)

弟弟和我一起玩。

提醒学生，这句话是以玲玲的
视角说的。

参考问题和答案：

1 Whose turn is it? (It is Hao Hao's turn.)

2 What is Brownie doing? (It is watching Hao Hao, Ling Ling and Dad playing the game.)

3 What is Mum doing? (She is taking some fruit out of a bag.)

妈妈快来，到你了。

参考问题和答案：

1　What are Hao Hao and Ling Ling doing? (They are calling Mum.)
2　Whose turn is it now? (It is Mum's turn.)
3　What is Brownie doing? (It is staring at the board game.)

谢谢妈妈!

参考问题和答案:

1 Why are the children so excited? (Because Mum is bringing them fruit.)
2 What is Brownie doing? (It is moving a piece on the board game.)

人们一般会把体型比较小的狗称作"小狗"。

gǒu
狗

小狗和我们一起玩。

参考问题和答案：

Brownie joins in the board game. Are the children enjoying it? How do you know? (Yes, they like playing the board game with Brownie because Hao Hao is giving it the thumbs up.)

Let's think

1 Recall the story and number the pictures in order. Write in Chinese.

四　　一　　三　　二

2 Recall the story and look at the pictures. Put a tick or a cross.

✗　　✓

✓　　✗

New words

1 Learn the new words.

狗

姐姐

弟弟

和

妈妈

爸爸

一起　玩

延伸活动：
学生用一句话描述妈妈、浩浩和玲玲。如：妈妈和小狗一起玩。/浩浩和玲玲一起玩。/姐姐和弟弟一起玩。

2 Draw lines to match the words to the pictures.
每个人物的路径都不只一种，学生只要将单词和人物正确配对即可。

爸爸　　弟弟　　姐姐　　狗　　妈妈

听听说说 Listen and say

第一题录音稿：
浩浩：姐姐，你几岁？
玲玲：我八岁。弟弟，你几岁？
浩浩：我六岁。
玲玲：小狗几岁？
浩浩：布朗尼一岁。

03 **1** Look, listen and match.

04 **2** Look at the pictures. Listen to the sto

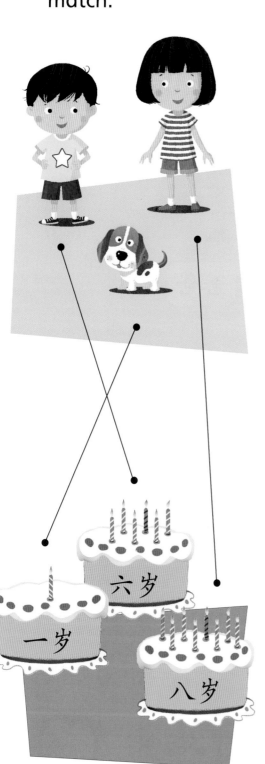

六岁

一岁

八岁

1 依森和艾文一起。

3 我和布朗尼一起。

nd say.

3 **Write the letters. Role-play with your friend.**

提醒学生根据第二题故事完成本题配对。

Task

Respond to the questions your friend asks. Draw a picture of your family.

你有姐姐/
弟弟吗?

她/他叫什
么名字?

她/他几岁?

游戏方法：
以"XX和XX"的句式说出两个角色名称，学生画路线连接两角色。每种角色搭配的行走
路线不只一种，只要正确连接所听到的两个角色即可。

Game

参考搭配：爸爸和艾文、浩浩和伊森、玲玲和布朗尼、
妈妈和爱莎。

Who are they going to meet?
Listen to your teacher and draw
the paths.

Song

🎧 **Listen and sing.**

我的家，

我的家，

有爸爸和妈妈，

有姐姐和弟弟，

还有小狗布朗尼。

延伸活动：

1 学生四人一组，分别扮演爸爸、妈妈、姐姐和弟弟的角色。

2 全班合唱第一、二、五行歌词，到第三、四行歌词停下，由老师独唱。

3 老师可自由搭配第三、四行歌词中的人物，学生配合做动作。如：老师唱"有爸爸和弟弟，有姐姐和妈妈"，则扮演爸爸和弟弟、姐姐和妈妈的两组学生分别互相击掌。

课堂用语 Classroom language

非常好。

Excellent.

排队。

Queue up.

围圆圈。

Form a circle.

 **写一写 Write**

1 **Learn and trace the stroke.**

老师示范笔画功夫，学生跟着做：双脚并拢，膝盖稍微向前弯曲，脚尖绷直点地。从左侧看过去，腿部的形状即为"撇点"的形状。

撇点

2 **Learn the component. Trace** 女 **to complete the characters.**

学生观察图片，引导他们发现女字旁与女性有关。

3 **Find the flowers with** 女 **inside. Colour them red and the others yellow.**

4 Trace and write the character.

ㄑ 夊 女 女「 妈 妈

妈 妈 妈

5 Write and say.

妈 妈

汉字小常识 Did you know?

Many components provide clues to how a character sounds.

Can you guess the pronunciation of the characters?

mǎ	mā	ma	mǎ	mà
马	妈	吗	码	骂

在带有形声部件的汉字中，有的字跟形声部件的读音完全相同，如"奶（nǎi）"和"乃（nǎi）"；有的声母、韵母相同，声调不同，如"妈（mā）"和"马（mǎ）"；还有的只有声母或韵母相同，如"绿（lǜ）"和"录（lù）"、"睛（jīng）"和"青（qīng）"；有的甚至读音完全不同，如"删（shān）"和"册（cè）"。

多元学习 Connections

Cultures

1 Look at the Chinese family tree. Circle the elder sister and the younger brother.

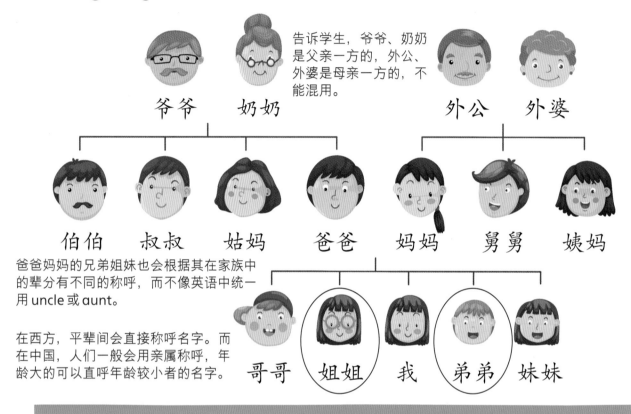

告诉学生，爷爷、奶奶是父亲一方的，外公、外婆是母亲一方的，不能混用。

爷爷　奶奶　　　　　外公　外婆

伯伯　叔叔　姑妈　爸爸　妈妈　舅舅　姨妈

爸爸妈妈的兄弟姐妹也会根据其在家族中的辈分有不同的称呼，而不像英语中统一用 uncle 或 aunt。

在西方，平辈间会直接称呼名字。而在中国，人们一般会用亲属称呼，年龄大的可以直呼年龄较小者的名字。

哥哥　姐姐　我　弟弟　妹妹

> Different kinship terms are used to show whether a family member is younger or older, or whether this person is on the father's side or mother's side.

2 Do you have these relatives? Circle the leaves if you do.

Mother's side			Father's side	
舅舅 mother's brother	uncle		father's elder brother	伯伯
			father's younger brother	叔叔
姨妈 mother's sister	aunt		father's sister	姑妈

Project

1 Make your family tree.

② 将家庭成员的照片用不干胶贴在树上。

③ 用彩笔画出家庭成员的关系。

① 材料：一棵硬卡纸做的小树、一支不干胶、几支彩笔、一把剪刀。

2 Show the family tree to your friend. Talk about your family.

我叫_____，我____岁。

我爸爸叫_____。

我妈妈叫_____。

我姐姐叫_____，她____岁。

我弟弟叫_____，他____岁。

1 Play with your friend. Choose a colour and complete the tasks on card A and card B in each round.

A

1

Say 'thank you' in Chinese.

谢谢

A

A

3

姐姐和弟弟一起玩。

A

A

2

我叫玲玲。

A

A

3

姐姐六岁。

A

B

3

What is the meaning?

The elder sister and the younger brother play together.

B

B

3

What is the question for A? Say in Chinese.

姐姐几岁？

B

B

1

Reply in Chinese.

不客气

B

B

1

Say the rest of the numbers up to ten.

二、四、六、八、十

B

评核方法：
学生两人一组，互相考察评价表内单词和句子的听说读写。交际沟通部分由老师朗读要求，学生再互相对话。如果达到了某项技能要求，则用色笔将星星或小辣椒涂色。

When you complete a task, you will get the mark(s) on the card.

A

1

一 三 五
七 九

B

2

What is the question for A? Say in Chinese.

你叫什么名字？

2 Work with your friend. Colour the stars and the chillies.

Words and sentences	说	读	写
爸爸	☆	☆	🌶
妈妈	☆	☆	☆
姐姐	☆	☆	🌶
弟弟	☆	☆	🌶
狗	☆	☆	🌶
和	☆	🌶	🌶
一起	☆	🌶	🌶
玩	☆	🌶	🌶
姐姐和弟弟一起玩。	☆	🌶	🌶

Address family members	☆

评核建议：

根据学生课堂表现，分别给予"太棒了！(Excellent!)"、"不错！(Good!)"或"继续努力！(Work harder!)"的评价，再让学生圈出左侧对应的表情，以记录自己的学习情况。

3 What does your teacher say?

My teacher says ...

21

分享 Sharing

Words I remember

爸爸	bà ba	father, dad
妈妈	mā ma	mother, mum
姐姐	jiě jie	elder sister
弟弟	dì di	younger brother
狗	gǒu	dog
和	hé	and

延伸活动：
1 学生用手遮盖英文，读中文单词，并思考单词意思；
2 学生用手遮盖中文单词，看着英文说出对应的中文单词；
3 学生两人一组，尽量运用中文单词分角色复述故事。

| 一起 | yī qǐ | together |
| 玩 | wán | to play |

Other words

| 我们 | wǒ men | we, us |
| 小 | xiǎo | small |

OXFORD
UNIVERSITY PRESS

Oxford University Press is a department of the University of Oxford.
It furthers the University's objective of excellence in research, scholarship,
and education by publishing worldwide. Oxford is a registered trade mark of
Oxford University Press in the UK and in certain other countries

Published in Hong Kong by
Oxford University Press (China) Limited
39th Floor, One Kowloon, 1 Wang Yuen Street, Kowloon Bay,
Hong Kong

© Oxford University Press (China) Limited 2017

The moral rights of the author have been asserted

First Edition published in 2017

Illustrated by Anne Lee and Wildman

Photographs for reproduction permitted by Dreamstime.com

China National Publications Import & Export (Group) Corporation is an authorized distributor of
Oxford Elementary Chinese.

Please contact content@cnpiec.com.cn or 86-10-65856782

ISBN: 978-0-19-082139-5

10 9 8 7 6 5 4

Teacher's Edition
ISBN: 978-0-19-082151-7

10 9 8 7 6 5 4 3 2